THE BEST NEWS
OF ALL TIME

Leonard Louis Brown

Published by Leonard Brown

THE BEST NEWS
OF ALL TIME

ISBN 978-0-9567354-0-9

First Published 2010 by

Leonard Brown

http://www.leonardbrown.org.uk

We were not given our unique brains and bodies to wage wars and cause endless destruction, or to commit the countless other multiplying and ever-worsening evils of our present way of life, all of which were necessary for us to reach this stage in our evolution. But nothing good is free and we had to learn by harsh experience what not to do before a way of life can be established in which no deliberate evils can be tolerated.

Our true purpose is to make this planet a paradise in which every normal child will have the best possible education and a constantly improving quality of life.

That time has come, as is made clear in the remarkably easy-to-read book.

IN MEMORIAM

The time has come to remember, shed copious tears for, and pay tribute to the countless millions of innocent people whose cruel exploitation, untold suffering, torture, and/or painful and premature death was the price that had to be paid to learn how to fulfil our true purpose in life. We could not otherwise have reached this stage in our evolution.

We must also remind ourselves that billions of people are still being cruelly exploited and/or destroyed, and that this will continue until all nations have adopted the wonderful way of life that can now be had for the first time.

CONTENTS

PREFACE

Accelerating technology was steadily improving the living standards and life quality for more and more people in all countries until the mid-1950's. It has since then been used to transfer our wealth to our rulers and make life worse for us.

Public servants have made themselves our immovable masters. The very rich grow richer; the rest of us grow poorer; the divide widens every day.

Only the greedy, self-serving elite can presently benefit from this dreadful way of life, but we have yet to learn that everything that has happened had to happen for us to reach this stage in our evolution and that no one can be blamed for what has happened. Without the strict disciplines, false beliefs, and dreadful exploitation of our present way of life we would still look and behave like our ape-like ancestors who emerged from primeval forests in the far distant past to conquer the world. Their only technology was flint tools and they had to search for food and shelter from dawn to dusk to survive.

We have made vast progress since then and could now easily satisfy every sensible person's demands, restore the environment, properly develop the latent talent of all children, and fulfil mankind's true purpose in life, if all people are employed to produce only the good things of life for their mutual benefit. But our rulers have made us believe that no other way of life be can be better, and so there had to be a dreadful crisis affecting everyone to make us sit up and take notice. The worldwide recession which became visible in 12005/6 has done the trick by ruining countless manufacturers and shop keepers, destroying tens of millions of jobs, and threatening the jobs of all workers in all industries, newspaper staff and broadcasters included.

Government taxes and food prices increase rapidly. Public spending power shrinks more every day. Life becomes more fearful, complex, chaotic and stressful. We have surrendered our collective voice, sit like dummies in front of the news broadcasts and the tabloids, and believe the latest spin that is pulling us down further into despair. We even believe our rulers when they tell us that their war in Iraq and Afghanistan, a war that costs the American and British taxpayers more than one billion dollars a day, is guarding against the tyranny of evil men who want to kill us and take our freedom!

WHAT FREEDOM? Our most precious freedoms have been destroyed. We are enslaved by a system of secrets and lies which serve only to line the pockets of those who contribute nothing to our quality of life.

How many more innocent lives must be lost?

How much destruction to our moral, to our economy, to our physical world, must we endure before we say, <u>enough</u>?

But things have come to a head. Hundreds of millions of people are becoming more and more angry, stressed, unhappy, disillusioned and desperate, and demand complete change in the way we are governed.

Why else would the Americans, the most negro-hating nation in the world, elect a Negro President? But they will soon learn that the fact that Obama's promises are no better than those of any other politician does not matter.

The door to the best possible way of life – a way that was forecast by Plato and Aristotle – is now easy to open. We now have all that is needed.

A *Non-Political All People's Party* can now be formed to contest all general elections in all parliamentary democracies with a mandate to put an end to politics and to secrecy, the root cause and protection of all evils, unite all nations, and make life improve for all people in all countries in line with technology that would increase very much faster than it can do now.

Landslide victories would be the order of the day and despots would very soon be deposed because this news cannot be suppressed. Thousands of millions of desperate and caring people will rally to the cause.

We are no longer evolving. We are more and more frightened, greedy, impaired, illiterate, unconscious, and wasteful. It is easy to prove that world economies collectively produce less than 3% of the good things of life that would be produced in the new way of life portrayed in the text that follows.

The very definition of prosperity has become totally corrupted. Making more money at other people's expense is now the sole purpose of every activity. We have forgotten that money was invented to make it easy to exchange different products and that money can buy nothing if we produce nothing. We have lost all sense of value and don't realize how poor and desperate we are now - lazy, unproductive, and debt-ridden.

But appearances are deceptive. For the first time we now have it within our power to turn it all around and make life improve faster and faster for all people everywhere. We can now have completely open world government by a newly formed Economic, Social, and Cultural Cooperative of which every person is a life member with an equal say in world affairs. Everyone could then see things as they are and know what best to do at all times.

There would be no more wars, hatreds, crime, suicide bombers, avoidable pollution, or mass destruction. The purpose of every activity would be to do it better, no matter how good it may be, bearing in mind that nothing can ever be perfect, that nothing good is free, and that without worthwhile challenges we would very soon become extinct.

Chapter 1

HOW FAR WE HAVE COME?

Very few people realise that education, living standards, culture and quality of life was steadily improving for nearly all people in all industrialised countries in line with fast accelerating technology until World War II broke out in 1939. Nearly everything produced or provided was better and cheaper every year. By 1937 a school teacher, or a reasonably well-paid British factory or office worker, or a good commercial traveller, could buy a well-built three-bedroom house with a garden in the rear for less than £500, even in London. It might even have a small garden in the front, but there would be no garage or domestic appliances. It was usually paid for by a 10% deposit and a ten-year mortgage, with an annual interest rate of not more than 4%, and the buyer could give a family with two or three children far better food, clothing, education, and quality life than can now be had by children of far richer families <u>without the wife or husband going to work</u>!

Long term mortgages with complex agreements and huge penalties did not exist. Educational grants for deserving scholars were readily available. Government restrictions were minimal and all government services were free.

Enterprising people in all non-communist countries could establish a useful business with minimal capital and nearly all employed people had endowment insurance policies. Premiums were paid to weekly collectors. More and more workers had a savings account. All government services were free and all public servants were our servants in the true sense of these words.

Technology has multiplied several thousand times since then, because every new thought or idea creates several more, each of which does the same in an endless sequence, and so among the many questions we should be asking are:

Why have we been made ignorant of these vital facts of a good life?

Why is everything worsening faster, instead of improving faster every day?

Why are two or three jobs necessary to keep our heads above water?

Why does our money buy less every day?

Why are our jobs increasingly stressful and insecure?

Why do so many of us have to work longer hours for less pay?

Why do so few of us get decent pensions?

Why are so many people in all countries living in dire poverty and misery?

Why have we allowed politicians, bureaucrats, and other so-called public servants, to become our grossly overpaid and undisputed masters? They make new laws and regulations, destroy hard won freedoms by bogus safety regulations and impose costly stealth taxes which serve only to make even the wealthiest people poorer and increasingly fearful of the future?

Why did our post World War II government transfer the industries that had been making life better for nearly all people every year to slave wage countries and make public education worsen visibly, when there is so much more to learn every day. Britain went far further than any other country in providing a better standard of living for its population, but Britain has since become a prime example of how it has all gone horribly wrong, with fast growing unemployment, shrinking spending power, rising taxes, and fast increasing prices of commodity goods.

They told everyone they had to make way for "high technology industries", but none of the so-called "industries" which replaced them is an industry in the true sense of this word. They create colossal waste, complexity, misery, ignorance, and suffering, and have made it almost impossible to see things as they are and know what best to do for ourselves and for all other people.

Millions of school leavers cannot do even the simplest addition, division, or multiplication, without a calculator! Few know anything about literature, the arts, culture, or any other of the countless good things of life.

Nor have they the slightest understanding of current affairs. But they do know far too much of what is bad for their own good and for the world at large. Were we not kept so ignorant and so busy trying to find a little pleasure in a world in which everyone seems to be trying to cheat one another and to get more for doing less work, it would be obvious that our undisputed masters are deliberately creating so much chaos, stress, and fear for our lives and for the future, that we will eventually beg for the *"security"* of an updated version of George Orwell's Big Brother Slave World.

They would tell each other how much better off they are than their long gone ancestors, there being no unemployed or wars, and everybody having a small warm home, three (junk) meals a day, free drugs, regular shopping buying rubbish, free trash TV programmes, and cheap short holidays. That their lives should be a million times better would not enter their ruined minds.

No one seems to know why this policy was adopted, but one thing seems clear: Despite commonplace technology that now enables us to access encyclopaedic knowledge at a touch of a computer keyboard, our leaders are doing their best to keep us ignorant of simple facts that could enable us to live a far better life. But the technology cannot be stopped, and it is our responsibility to use it on a mass scale for effective purposes.

Some of us now realise that we are fast approaching the stage in our evolution in which it should be easy to impose the will and fundamental need, of the masses, and spread it more and more evenly, in line with this fast improving technology. We know we can readily communicate and spread ideas on a global scale. We must now realise that we can now fulfil our true purpose in life and take our lead from other living creatures, those without the intellectual facilities we take for granted, and who evolve instinctively.

We must wake up to the fact that money can buy nothing if we produce nothing. Only a tiny fraction of the world's employed people are producing the necessities and luxuries of a good life in factories that are collectively not nearly as productive as they should be. Their output is only a tiny fraction of what it could be if all people were usefully employed.

In other words, waste is winning the day. Far too much goes to those who provide or produce nothing that should feed or house, clothe, properly educate, or help us in any way. We spend billions of dollars on war and make film stars, sports-people, their managers, sponsors, and other "celebrities" multi millionaires and worship them like gods. We have completely lost sight of what has intrinsic value and waste what little money and resources we have on things that numb us and dumb us down - which is precisely how our leaders want us to be.

In bygone days entertainers were glad to entertain us in return for simple board and lodging. Professional footballers were glad to get a factory-worker's pay, rather than suffer the tedium of factory work.

We pay outrageous sums of money to those who only serve to cram our minds with useless distractions,

Teachers, nurses, social workers, emergency servicemen and women, factory workers are grossly underpaid.

Millions of shops and other small businesses have been bankrupted. More and more large companies are merging, creating behemoth monopolies with an ability to undercut small businesses and strangle competition.

Supermarkets are forced to sell foods for less, but they are quick to sacrifice quality for the sake of profit. Those of us who are looking for healthy, nutritious foods must spend more in relative terms than ever before.

Man-made drugs and inoculations compromise our long-term health in favour of a 'quick-fix,' and the greatest irony being that we stay on these drugs, go back for more, and become increasingly dependent on them to stay alive.

Millions of us who should be healthy, active, and productive are being left behind – dependent on prescribed medications and all manner of distractions that keep us from any reasonable standard of living.

Chapter 2

WHERE WE NEED TO GO

Despite all this doom and gloom, we have reached a time in our evolution at which a world wide *Non-political All People's Party* can unite the world, eradicate secrecy and politics, and make everything improve in line with incredibly fast increasing knowledge of what is good and bad for us.

The sole purpose of ever human activity would always be to make it better, no matter how good it may be, and all nations would help one another to diversify their industries and to make their economies as productive, diversified, and self-sufficient as possible without payment of any kind.

All school leavers and graduates would have the widest possible choice of challenging careers, and everyone would be employed to produce or provide as much as possible of only the good things of life.

There would soon be more than enough to satisfy the ever growing demands of all sensible people. Restoring the natural environment and climate would be a top priority.

Far fewer irreplaceable natural resources would be used, because everything produced would be the best quality possible at any given time, it would last very much longer, and people would have far better taste. We would waste as little as possible, make no munitions, and try not to harm anyone in any way. Deliberate crime would not be tolerated.

Not only would technology increase many times faster than it can now, but a keen awareness, borne out of social responsibility and unity, of what is good and what is bad for us, would make the transition far easier than now seems possible.

Well qualified candidates would be chosen by a lottery system, comprised of an abundant supply of able-bodied applicants. Having served their time, all officials would be well rewarded, given different work without loss of pay, and replaced by others chosen in the same way.

What matters most in our present way of life is not what you know, but who you know, but this would no longer apply. Truth, openness, and mutual aid in all functions of life would become instinctive in all functions of life, and self-serving hierarchies would become a mere historical footnote.

Progress would be slow for only a few years. Mistakes will be made, but improvement will very soon be very much faster than now seems possible because everything we do creates more of the same kind.

In the absence of obstacles such as patents and copyright, and secrecy, worst of all, the output of good things will be much faster than now seems possible and very much sooner.

Lies and false beliefs that have been drilled into us by repetition from infancy to old age will surface from time to time, but this would not make very much difference. But it must of course be understood that even though our lives will very soon be transformed, the full benefits cannot begin to flow until a new generation is properly educated.

Nothing can be perfect, but all rational people will gladly settle for a life that improves faster every year, knowing that this is the beginning of a peaceful transition that may take three, four or five decades to complete.

Everyone would also know that they would be fulfilling their true purpose in life, as do all other living creatures instinctively.

Every species, other than mankind, instinctively makes the best use it can of the resources available in its environment. It adapts to changing conditions in a constantly changing world, or it becomes extinct. It improves by natural selection and by learning where to find more or better food and natural remedies. It limits its population to the number that can be supported in its environment. and it plays its part in maintaining a clean and self-balancing environment that improves imperceptibly – until we interfere!

But whereas no other species can destroy its environment or make it improve faster, we can now make this planet unfit for human and animal life for hundreds of millions of years by pressing a few switches and creating a massive nuclear holocaust, or we can use incredibly fast growing technology to make this planet an every-improving Paradise well within the lifetime of a normal child, or we can allow our villainous rulers to make us ignorant slaves, as has already been stated.

That choice is ours. What do you want?

Chapter 3

THE GOAL OF A WORLD CO-OPERATIVE

There would be true co-operation throughout the world between all people in all walks of life.

There would be no war, terrorism, suicide bombing, or military action of any other kind. Explosives would be used only for necessary projects.

All nationalised industries and services would be transferred to the Co-operative and integrated. Industries and services that are not already nationalised would be acquired at a sensible valuation, as and when this is convenient.

All research would be integrated and used to benefit all nations.

Useless jobs and services would be history. There would be no politicians, career bureaucrats, speculators, criminals, lawyers, financial advisers, or cunning parasites of infinite variety, all of whom would have far better things to do. There would be no traffic wardens or other collectors of stealth taxes.

Entertainers, sports people and other so called celebrities would no longer be obscenely overpaid and put on pedestals. Nor would they fill the media with accounts of their hugely expensive ways of life. One talent is worth no more than another, and even in the case where one's profession actually contributes a great deal to human well-being, one's salary would never dwarf the salary of someone who, say, provided basic services.

Fast increasing productivity would reduce working hours and provide an abundance of spare time to engage with all manner of free cultural and physical leisure facilities. As a result, people would be healthier and happier, and therefore reduce the burden on the healthcare system.

Nearly all people would be active until they were very old. All employable people would have secure and satisfying employment, and a pension that maintains a quality of life.

Mothers of young children could choose to be employed, subject to their children being properly cared for without any compromise, to child or mother.

All care, other than nursing, would be a part time duty for everyone.

Inflation would be replaced by deflation. Everything would constantly improve and cost less to make and distribute. Everyone would have so much more spending power that no one would need loans and all sensible people could be free from crippling debt. Personal loans, credit card debts and mortgages could be repaid by a very simple tax system without harming living standards.

Education would not be used to destroy our minds, as it does now. It would truly enable children to discover and develop their latent talents. Every normal child has enormous talent potential. An immense wealth of bright, talented, creative young people would contribute in all manner to a human race sincerely vested in its growth and development – in the arts, culture, industry, environment, technology, co-operation.

Better education would improve our quality of life and we would use the time gained from greater productivity and better health to appreciate good music, good food, good literature, good art, and the many other good things of life. Schools would have wide ranging sports and cultural facilities that would also serve the greater community beyond regular school hours.

Higher education would be the norm, and more and more people of all ages would be discovering and developing their latent talents.

People's needs would be easily seen and catered for, even by people from different areas and countries, and a simple code of ethical practice would very soon apply throughout the world.

Water would be piped from where it is plentiful to wherever it is needed. Deserts would be made fertile. Lost forests would be replaced or replanted elsewhere, and this depletion of the earth's oxygen supply would be brought back into check. The seasons would eventually become normal and change only in accordance with the natural order.

Hundreds of millions of poverty stricken people now living in shanty towns and in appalling conditions in overpopulated cities, such as Mexico City, would be transferred to new towns and properly housed and trained to do useful work. This planet can easily support its present population.

There would be no profit taxes, income taxes, stealth taxes, council taxes, industrial premises taxes, or taxes on vehicles or any other products or services. One standard tax on all spending and on inherited wealth would take a much smaller part of far greater public spending power, and yet this would provide constantly improving government and public services, all of which would be free. These would eventually include insurance, all public transport, and the many other essential services we now pay for heavily.

Everything produced would be the best quality and would be sold at the lowest commercial price.

We would no longer make unnatural medications or use inoculations with animal serums or hormones. All medications would conform to nature and fulfil their proper purpose and we would no longer create new diseases which may be incurable, or make traditional diseases more virulent, as we do now.

Fewer and fewer people would be in wheel chairs or suffer from cancer or any other deadly disease, and nearly all people would live much longer and be active until they die.

Integrated medical research would be primarily for prevention of disease, or for better natural remedies, or for better methods of surgery. Precision instruments we can only dream about would be commonplace.

Competent medical practitioners, nurses, and necessary administrators would provide the highest possible quality health care on demand.

All farming would be made organic as quickly as possible and all food would be healthy.

Fewer and fewer laws, law enforcers, and restrictions on freedoms would be needed because all people all people would behave more responsibly.

Simply worded local laws, rules and regulations would be designed to suit local requirements, none of which would be enforced when it is not necessary. Everyone would be held responsible for everything they do.

All prisons would be fully self supporting and crime would rapidly reduce. Even the smallest deliberate crimes would be so severely penalised that they would very soon no longer be committed by normal people.

Religions would join in the common purpose of promoting the concept of mutual help and maximising productivity of whatever makes life better.

Millions of exiles would return to their homelands and rejoin their families and friends.

These are only a few of the countless benefits of a World Unifying Party.

Chapter 4

THE TRUE PURPOSE OF RELIGION

The true purpose of religion must surely be to unite people through a common vision of tolerance, benevolence and compassion.

We have misunderstood this purpose, with disastrous results.

Islamic fundamentalists forbid "non-believers" to enter their mosques and declare that theirs is the only true religion. Those who refuse to convert should be killed.

The Spanish Inquisition, the Holocaust, the war in the former Yugoslavia, the enforced conversion to Christianity in South America, the endless, bloody dispute between Palestinian Arabs and Israeli Jews, the ethnic genocide in Rwanda, and so much more murder and corruption: all this dreadful villainy in the name of God! What has happened to our common sense?

It should be obvious by now that religions, as they are presently taught and practised, are the oldest, most successful and destructive confidence tricks of all time, but they were the product of their time and were necessary until we reached this stage in our evolution.

This would all change. People would be squarely focused on what is right for themselves and what is right for every man, woman and child.

Honest clerics would tell us that the Hebrew Bible clearly states that its content is only the beginning of knowledge; that our duty is to gather more and more knowledge, educate our children properly, and do unto others as we would have them to do onto us

This command, which summarises the true purpose of religion, is omitted from the Ten Commandments in all scriptures because children are not taught to be masters by devilish rulers who want us all to be ignorant slaves.

They use fear and hatred to keep us dependent. Religion is a tried and tested devise to distract our attention from the true purpose of life.

Religious division is some of the best propaganda man has ever devised to drive people crazy with fear and hatred, to keep us locked in our homes, under their "protection".

How can we be blamed? We have been dis-empowered. We don't know how to take of ourselves.

We should know by now that the universal belief in a human-like Creator was a necessary stage in our evolution, but we now know that this is obviously no longer necessary.

The beautiful miracle of this planet is technological perfection on a scale that cannot be matched by anything man-made. If we did indeed have the intelligence to create this planet, then we would not be systematically destroying it, as we are doing.

It is patently obvious that we haven't come close to our true potential, which is to live harmoniously and compliment this great miracle, rather than slap it in the face.

If we are indeed the intelligent specie our religions tell us we are, then we would turn this train wreck around and get on the right path.

All clerics in all religions should now join hands with genuine social reformers and producers and distributors of the good things of life, and fulfil the true purpose of religion. As stated earlier, this must surely be to do everything possible to unite people and do what is best for mankind and all other living creatures.

Chapter 5

DOWN WITH SECRECY!

Secrecy is unavoidable when resources are in short supply. People who know where they can find a scarce resource do not tell others without getting paid. Those of us who possess particular insights and/or skills that enable us to procure scarce resources will only sell their insights and/or skills for a great deal of money. For those individuals or companies who pay handsomely for these insights and/or skills, it is unthinkable that they themselves will give up these insights and/or skills for anything less than a profit. They will naturally guard against others attaining their insight and/or skills as best hey can. The paradigm of greed perpetuates this cycle. Secrecy is their tool.

In a world that produces all that is needed to satisfy every person's demands, there will be no need for what is best described as badly motivated greed and no place for secrecy.

We are fortunate in that we have reached the stage in our evolution where we have sufficient technology, skills, understanding, and experience to produce a growing abundance of all that is needed to satisfy all people's needs. Ours is the luckiest of all generations, did we but know it.

If our affairs are honestly and efficiently managed in a completely open society, no information that could help or harm anyone would be kept secret. Any deliberate infringement, no matter how small, would be severely punished and no one would dare commit an offence.

We are currently saddled with an ever-growing army of regulators and enforcers who are very clearly doing nothing to help alleviate the greed and corruption that is making life more and more difficult all the time. They are enforcing regulations and restrictions that only perpetuate the misery, and we are only hearing about their folly when it is too late. Under a World Unifying Party, these regulators and enforcers will be employed for the mutual benefit of all people everywhere, and they themselves will be regulated by a world that is without secrecy.

We believe what we are taught to believe. Ancient beliefs, lies, and misconceptions that are taught from birth, for hundreds of thousands of years, and which are repeated constantly, become never-questioned truths. Only openness in all things can remedy this situation, and slowly unravel the web of misconceptions about survival we have come to believe in.

We have the wherewithal to eradicate secrecy by dismantling the compulsion of badly motivated greed. We can live in a world where greed is properly motivated because there is enough for everyone, and there is no need to horde the good things in life. Greed would then make us want to make everything even better than it is for everyone's benefit.

Chapter 6

DUMB DOWN OR SMARTEN UP: EDUCATION

Every normal child has a talent that may be true genius, nearly all of which is smothered by a public education system that is hopelessly underfunded and undervalued.

Our brains can store an enormous amount of useful knowledge, but they are filled with rubbish, because universal ignorance of the economic and ethical realities of life is now the only way our rulers can retain and increase their immense power and privilege.

The British people know only what their rulers allow them to know and are now amongst the worst educated of all industrialised nations. A growing majority cannot read, spell, speak, or write properly. They cannot add, subtract or multiply two or three single digit numbers without a calculator. Very few know anything about good literature, good culture, good music, the true facts of history, or the many other good things of life.

Very little education was needed when technology was primitive and shortages were unavoidable. Education's underlying purpose must now be to create a society in which people are educated! Educated people who are taught to appreciate the good things of life behave responsibly and make the best contribution they can for everyone's mutual benefit.

Under a unified world cooperative, every nation will have a sufficient variety of industries to provide challenging careers for all school leavers and graduates. The best and widest possible education would then be essential because there would be so much more to learn than ever before.

Some children are far more academic and love to learn. Some dislike academic work and are better suited to acquiring technical skills. But these demands could easily be met, and with utmost efficiency, in a world of abundance.

People would store as much useful knowledge as need be and question everything to make sure they know its true meaning and purpose. It would then be easy to make the best use of their ability for the mutual benefit of all people.

Experience proves that learning by rote how to read, calculate, write, spell, punctuate, and speak fluently, gives most children the confidence, desire and ability to learn more. The more they learn, the more they want to learn, and the easier it becomes to learn more. Formal education should therefore begin at the earliest age possible and continue for as long as necessary.

This is not as difficult as it may seem because technology now makes this very much easier than it was in the past. More could now be learned about rich culture, for example, than was ever before possible.

In the past, before we had all this amazing technology that brings the magic of the universe to our fingertips, we spent many days visiting galleries, museums and places of cultural significance. In a world that puts the focus back onto appreciation of the good things in life, the way children use technology would be much different. As it is, technology and enforced disciplines are used to create ignorant, flag-waving hooligans who are too bored and uneducated to know their lives could be far better. But even the best education may be wasted, if children are undisciplined, unhappy, worried, unduly stressed, or badly brought up.

Everyone must learn the over-riding importance of truth, sensible discipline and other basic facts of a good life, and why they must always try to do better. We must also know why privileges and freedoms must not be taken for granted or used to mistreat others. We must know why good food is essential for good physical and mental health, and why all medications should be natural.

Single sex schools large enough to adopt the House System of most traditional British Public Boarding Schools for ten-year-olds and upwards would help concentrate the mind without the distractions of sex. This would also encourage healthy competition, and make it easier to cater for significant differences in learning ability. Putting the slow with the average and the very bright frustrates all groups. Fluency in two or three foreign languages would be the norm, with appropriate subjects taught in these languages to encourage thinking in them. Examinations and worthwhile prizes for outstanding achievement would be standard practice. Why should education differ from sporting activities or entertainment? Personal responsibility and minimal paper work would be the rule in all things. Parents would discuss their children's needs and progress with teachers on a regular basis. Films showing the deadly effects of narcotics addiction would be shown periodically to make absolutely sure their dreadful dangers are common knowledge

All pupils should be encouraged to play the piano. This versatile instrument makes it easier to appreciate good music and learn how to play the instruments they like best. Inherent genius may show early, given the right environment, but aptitudes are not as essential for the enjoyment and understanding of good music or to enjoy playing or performing as is generally supposed. A famous Japanese teacher named Suzuki taught himself to play the violin as a child and devised methods that enabled thousands of young children with little or no apparent talent to become proficient violinists.

It is reasonable to suppose that this would apply to all musical instruments.

Learning good poetry, reading good literature and engaging in a variety of cultural activities, including mind-developing games such as chess and bridge, would be given the importance they deserve.

Computers and computer games, the misuse of which is largely responsible for falling standards everywhere, would be strictly controlled until sufficient experience and knowledge is acquired to use them wisely.

Rapidly developing technology would inevitably make job changing much more frequent and compel nearly all primary schools to have a common syllabus. Children would otherwise be disadvantaged when parents move home. A longer school day would allow ample time for sports, athletics, swimming, nature study courses and a variety of worthwhile cultural activities. Children could walk to school and all other destinations safely.

Schools and universities would have comprehensive indoor and outdoor sports, cultural and other leisure facilities for use by local communities after school hours, even in rural areas. The syllabus for university students would allow them to take part time jobs in industry and be independent of parental help. This would make them more aware of the economic realities of life, but even this would eventually be unnecessary.

All able bodied people should do routine jobs in factories for a year or more before embarking on their chosen careers, most of which would change several times before they retire. Diversity and the widest possible experience are the essence of freedom.

Productive industries would provide a far wider choice of satisfying and well paid careers than professions and all earnings would be proportional to the contribution made to society until money is no longer needed or used.

Most students would choose careers in industry, farming, or restoring the environment, or researching more efficient ways of producing non-polluting energy and natural remedies. The traditional stigma of factory work would be replaced by a proper appreciation of the value of the textiles, clothing, footwear, furniture, and the many other products we use in our daily lives.

Most workers would be as literate, well read and cultured as teachers and other professionals. Apprentice-type courses combining industrial training with classroom theory would be commonplace.

But the most important of all knowledge for all children is to know that they must ask questions about anything they need to know until they know the correct answer, and to never stop learning or questioning. There is always more to learn and question until we die.

This is yet another of the countless benefits of a World Unifying Party.

Chapter 7

THE TRUTH OF ECONOMICS & WORLD ECONOMIES

Good sense tells us that all nations must now join in the common purpose of making the best use possible of all our natural resources and of the skills and experience of all able bodied people for the mutual benefit of mankind and all other species. The true purpose of economics is to help us do this.

Less than one quarter of every nation's employable population could easily provide the best possible education, health care, public transport, and all other essential services. More than three quarters could produce an ever-growing abundance of the good things of life, and no one could profit at other people's expense, tell lies, or act corruptly in public or private affairs without this being quickly seen and remedied. Every nation's economy would provide the widest possible choice of challenging and fulfilling careers.

Compare this with the present economic situation in Britain.

Out of every twenty employable people:

__One__ is producing food, or working in one of our other few non-defence industries which are collectively not half as productive as they should be.

__One__ is producing or researching immensely expensive and deadly weapons for defence against fictitious enemies, or is researching genetic foods that defy nature, or is developing, researching or producing synthetic drugs and inoculations that weaken our immune system, destroy our intelligence, make us old, infirm, and dependent on mobility aids long before our time, and are now creating new diseases for which there are no known remedies,

Eighteen are providing ever worsening public services, or they are producing little or nothing of value, or they are enforcing more and more restrictions on valuable freedoms, or they are living on government handouts. The enormous cost of all this is paid by taxpayers!

Try to imagine what these people could produce if they are properly educated, trained and employed, and how much less tax would be needed by government! And yet this colossal waste is not the full amount.

To this must be added the production potential of at least two million retired people who would like to work but are not allowed to work.

To make a dreadful situation even worse, the average earnings of those who contribute little or nothing to public welfare is three, four or possibly five times more than the highest paid workers who produce the things we need for a good life.

Earnings, such as those of top footballers and other entertainers, defy all logic, as do bonuses for financial advisers and stock exchange staff and top executives. These may be measured in millions of pounds or their equivalent in other currencies, a disease that is rapidly spreading in nearly all countries, but there is still much more and worse to come!

Very few school leavers and university students can have useful careers because we have lost so many useful industries. And so more and more useless jobs are created to make us believe the economy is doing well, but everyone can now see that public spending power is shrinking faster and faster and that their future is increasingly fearful.

Nothing like this could happen if all people could see things as they are. They would know that in a completely open society very few of us would be needed to keep accounts, advertise products and services, or to do the countless other time consuming, unproductive jobs demanded by the present system. Hundreds of millions of useful people would be free to acquire new skills and make a fast growing contribution to public well-being.

Public services would be as efficient as technology and openness allow, but nothing can be changed overnight.

Pay differentials would steadily reduce, as more and more people become better educated and increasingly productive. Money would eventually not be needed and all nations would have much the same living standards and quality of life, while retaining their unique culture.

Governments would no longer invent fraudulent definitions and publish statistics that tell us economies are doing well, when they are worsening.

The Gross National Product or GNP is a typical example. This used to be a commonplace indicator for the average man to show what the economy produced, and how much it cost to manage the nation's affairs and provide essential public services. It made it easy to compare the efficiency of the economies of all nations. But this statistic is no longer published because the industries that improved our lives have mostly been transferred to cheap labour countries. If it were published it would show how little we produce and how dependent we are on exports of munitions and deadly drugs, and on cheap imports. Our economists were therefore instructed to conceal this villainy by changing the statistic.

The size of every nation's economy, the so-called GDP, is measured by the nation's total income, regardless of what the people are doing in return for the money they receive.

Nothing can be more misleading. The original statistic set out the amount and value of the food and manufactures produced by the nation's economy, including all the costs of production on one side of the ledger. The total cost of local and national government and all essential services that are paid for by taxpayers were set out on the opposite pages.

The total difference was the increase or decrease in the total value of the nation's assets during the previous year.

All government costs are now shown as a contribution to our economy on one side of the budget ledger, and as an expense on the other side. Everything we do is given a false value which prevents our seeing the true value of what is being created – which is far less in terms of what's good for us than the powers-that-be would have us think.

Industries which produce the necessities of life may appear to have far less value than football clubs whose sole assets is the value of their playing grounds and buildings after allowing for all debts. The City of London's economy provides only financial services; Britain's economy produces very little real wealth; and yet eminent experts stated that the City of London's economy is worth more than Russia's vast land, constructions, minerals, forests and oil deposits, and that Britain's economy is worth more than China's!

This makes us believe we are doing well, whereas the original and honest statistic would clearly tell us that the nation is getting poorer every day and that the financiers and Mafia and usurers and ruthless exploiters who now own or control this planet's land and other resources which should all be public property, get richer and richer at our expense. And so whereas everything was getting cheaper and better every year, everything now becomes more expensive: the quality is worse than it was before.

Petrol, for example, is in money terms about 120 times more expensive than when the author began driving in 1936! Vegetables and most other foods are on about the same level. Good restaurant food has increased even more. Government services that were all free are now charged for at extortionate rates. More and more restrictions demanding enormous payments are invented every year and administered by people whose salaries and expenses are paid by taxpayers. A vicious spiral has been created which reduces public spending power faster every year, whilst making everything more expensive to buy!

Whereas, the greater part of Japan's National Income and Gross National Product is from engineering and other useful products, Britain's pitifully few manufacturing industries produce mainly munitions for defence against fictitious enemies and drugs that make us old and infirm before our time. The greater part of our National Income is derived from sports, entertainment, financial advisers, insurers, money lenders, overseas investments, stealth taxes, and countless other money-making activities, none of which produces anything worthwhile and is reflected in constantly shrinking spending power, fast increasing taxes and waste, and rapidly worsening living standards.

The present statistic hides more and more waste and proves conclusively that economists do more damage to society in one day than negligent train drivers and drunken car drivers could do in a million years.

The world's industrialized economy is becoming more and more like a gigantic and worthless bubble. Soon enough it will collapse, especially when we run out of fossil fuels and chaos ensues.

In a true democratic world economists would have a proper sense of relative values. They would compare the workings of different producers or providers of similar products or services and use this information to make all producers more efficient. We could readily determine labour requirements, materials, energy, and other expenses required by similar enterprises to produce or provide a given end product or service, and make it easy to compare their relative efficiency.

Innovators, designers, authors, composers, musicians, sculptors, artists and others would not worry about how to put a roof over their heads.

The free exchange of information and constant search for better methods and better products would produce an endless supply of new ideas, and all products would incorporate the latest technology.

Annual increases in productivity would be customary. Even present day incomes would buy several times more products that are at least as good as the best now on sale. It would eventually be more convenient to take what we need and recycle all non-consumable products when they are no longer wanted.

The enormous economic damage caused by today's government policies is disguised by creating more and more useless jobs, the result of which is a proliferation of so called 'high technology' advisory and other so-called services, collectively known as the **'new economy'**, none of which produces anything useful.

The colossal waste and inevitable suffering is partly hidden by the fact that weapons and drugs are now so complex and profitable that exports of a given value will buy up to ten times more true value of imports of consumer and technical products from low wage countries.

Our economists tell us this is as it should be!

It should be increasingly obvious that all industrialists are now as threatened as their workers, but very few can yet see the purpose of what is happening, or know how much better and how much more profitable our industries would be, or how much happier and better off they would be themselves, if our affairs are properly managed.

Many good small businesses close down every day. Even global scale industries and commercial service providers are being undermined. Only monopoly industries are still doing reasonably well because they can charge what they like, but demands must steadily reduce, no matter what they do, or how much they spend on advertising - **until the system is replaced**.

More and more producers of all sizes will go to the wall, as world economies become more and more unbalanced. But they would be profitable and busy throughout the year in the new order. Those that cannot make the grade would be adequately compensated.

All research would be integrated internationally and financed publicly, with all findings freely available for universal use. More could be accomplished in weeks than would now take as many years.

Eminent physicists are convinced, for example, that abundant safe nuclear energy, low cost solar energy, and several other renewable forms of energy could be had within a few years, if we all worked together. Fossil fuels would be used mainly to produce plastics, chemicals and other useful materials.

Imports would eventually be limited to products that cannot be produced efficiently at home, or to provide more variety. These would be paid for by exports of surplus products or tourism.

With constantly improving education, and quality of life, people will want fewer material products and will spend much more time pursuing cultural activities. The majority of industries would produce the required equipment and would use far less irreplaceable resources than we use now.

Government and other taxes vary from country to country, but it can easily be proved that the amount stated in government statistics is very much less than the amount we pay. Statistics in 2005 stated that the amount taken of what we earn was about 37%.

If the term tax includes any cost that would not be incurred if our economies are properly managed and factories are equipped with the latest machinery, the true figure is more than 95% of pitifully low incomes,.

Big earners employ tax avoidance experts and pay a small fraction of what they would otherwise pay. We unknowingly pay their advisers. The inevitable result is that:

- Most products now cost far more to distribute than they cost to produce.
- Far more is now spent on advertising and packaging than on production.
- More is spent on administration in health services than on treatment.
- Patents and copyright can increase a selling price ten fold or more.
- Interest charges and penalties take more and more every day
- Government services are charged for even though we pay the salaries and expenses of their providers!
- Privatisation makes everything more expensive and less efficient.
- Our industries are easily not half as productive as they should be.

This chaos-creating vicious spiral continues unchecked because nearly everyone has lost all sense of value, responsibility, and fair play. No one has the slightest idea of what life could be like if openness is standard practice.

Banking would be free. All purchases would be charged to the buyer's account directly until money is no longer needed. We would all own everything we use, but no one would own land or other natural resources.

Insurance, the biggest of all service industries, would be a free government service. The savings on this alone would be enormous. Premiums must now cover the cost of advertising, marketing and keeping accounts, of commissions, salaries and expenses, of huge bonuses and pensions for top executives, of dividends for shareholders, of pensions for staff, and of assessing and paying insurance claims. Most of this could be slashed.

The cost to taxpayers for verifying and repairing or replacing insured property could be less than a quarter of what we now pay. Multi-million pound compensation claims for individuals would be bad memories. Expensive litigation would not be needed. Personal injuries would be dealt with by the health service. Homes would be far better protected against damage. Crime would be non-existent. Lost property would be restored to owners by the system.

People would live close to where they work and vastly reduce the waste, inefficiency, and frustration of commuting traffic.

Far better roads would eliminate nearly all traffic jams; vehicles would be no larger than necessary and use far less fuel.

Four or five decades would see most cities completely rebuilt, but building for indefinite use would probably be limited to carefully selected constructions that are widely accepted as being outstanding works of art and preserved for posterity.

Many services not yet thought of would be free, but all this and very much more can be had only if we put an end to avoidable waste.

Try to imagine what life would have been like for the masses, if the labour used to build the pyramids and tombs for royalty, the temples and cathedrals for fictitious Gods, and the castles and manors for royalty and aristocracy, had been used instead to make their lives better! The masses worked all hours but had less than 5% of the total wealth produced. More than 95% went to their rulers, priests, officials and landowners!

Has anything changed?

Little thought is needed to see where our best interests lie.

This is yet another of the countless benefits of a World Unifying Party.

Chapter 8

THE TRUTH ABOUT POLITICS & BUREAUCRACY

The power, influence and priceless connections of leading politicians give them so much more wealth and privilege than they would otherwise obtain in the private sector. They are not in it for the good of their constituents. They do what is best for politicians, pretending they are doing their best for their constituents, and have made politics the most corrupt of all professions.

But it must be clearly understood that all top politicians and leaders in all important activities are pre-selected by our hidden rulers before they are allowed to stand for election, and that they must do as they are told or lose their positions. They are puppets of a relative handful of powerful people who control or own most of the world's banks, media, insurance, food and drug conglomerates, land, oil reserves, mines, forests, and natural resources. They must do as they are told or lose the power and prestige that go with the job. False promises and legalised bribes to voters to get elected are therefore standard practice and are never questioned.

Political corruption is the theme of thousands of best selling novels, but names are quoted only if there is no risk of libel action, or if the potential legal costs are justified by increased sales. Political conniving is admitted even in autobiographies for which top politicians are paid immense sums of money, but this serves only to maintain the fiction of a free press and a free society.

The mass media do nothing to prevent this corruption because they are still party to what must be the most evil conspiracy of all time. That our elected politicians in the House of Commons must refer to each other as the Honourable or Right Honourable Member is no longer just a sad irony. Our freedom – the most important of all our possessions - is now at stake.

Politicians constantly disagree with one another, and pretend they know what's best for us. But they are all just jockeying for power and will grab power at any cost. They know also that they will be well looked after if they conform, even if they lose an election. Everything is so fickle and pragmatic in politics. They readily change parties to get nearer to the power they covet, knowing that the closer they are the more lucrative are the connections.

But even the most humble amongst them do far better than they could in any other profession. What matters most is not <u>what</u> you know, but <u>who</u> you know. Villains who know the right people can do as they please.

Political connections promote a host of extremely lucrative non-political careers. Politicians are winners, no matter how useless they are. Ministers can hire the best brains in the world, but they must only have good memories, be good actors, and have the cunning of the devil.

Our leaders, aided and abetted by the bureaucracy, have won complete control by stealth of government, the economy, all public services, and the entire nation's wealth. And as everything generates many times more of its own kind faster and faster, our legal system, economy, education system, mass media, farming, health care, public services and all our other activities are increasingly corrupted, inefficient, and diseased.

We now produce less and less of the things we need and employ more and more officials to invent more and more complexity and enforce more and more restrictions on freedoms. Their considerable salaries, administration costs, expenses and pensions are all paid by taxpayers whose purchasing power is constantly reducing.

Huge and constantly increasing fines are imposed for infringing regulations and restrictions that could not exist in a democratic society. Very large licence fees and other charges for government services which were previously paid for by government are now stealth taxes that are not shown in tax statistics and could not be levied in a democratic world!

It is noticeable that whereas those laws that become effective with minimal delay if they increase government revenues, or destroy hard-won freedoms, or enrich politicians, bureaucrats or powerful vested interests, the laws that would improve our lives take years to pass and invariably end up doing more harm than good.

Elected politicians and career civil servants who describe themselves as Public Servants are now our unchallenged masters who make their own rules, fix their own salaries, expenses, pensions and working conditions. They then charge this all back to their true masters, the general public, and they can be replaced only by others like them! The bureaucracy, police, and all others who serve the government in any way must do likewise or lose their far better status and living standards.

The time has come to ask our rulers: "Should our servants do as they please with our wealth, make us do what suits them best, or conceal even the most crucial and damaging information until we can do nothing to remedy the situation?"

Top politicians and the Lord Chief Justice live rent free or at negligible cost in palatial accommodations and spend millions of pounds of our money on prestigious homes and offices without consulting us. Red carpets are laid everywhere. They have suites in the most expensive hotels, the finest food and the most expensive vintage wines and cigars at our expense, but they eat the junk food of the common man when they do their rounds.

Not for them are the customs delays and tedium of package tours.

Nor do they wait for buses and trains that rarely arrive on time, suffer the misery of overcrowding and endless traffic jams, stand in the rain and cold at bus stops without shelters, or suffer the many other hazards of outdated public transport and badly maintained and overcrowded roads which should have been modernised ages ago.

Free executive aircraft and helicopters are at their disposal. Holidays by courtesy of wealthy beneficiaries of politics which few of us can afford are theirs for the asking. Obscene insult is added to endless injury by fostering wars and providing shelter for themselves in nuclear weapon proof bunkers.

Fraudulent statistics and false claims are everyday practice.

Political leaders get immense fees for worthless books, attending charity functions, and making so-called lecture tours that tell us nothing we don't know. They also provide multi million pound pension funds for themselves.

We pay the cost of their villainy and suffer the consequences.

They get all this and very much more for creating chaos and misery and betraying the Trusteeship of our Planet. Their policies are the worst and most effective form of terrorism because it is invisible. What better proof can there be that we have lost all sense of right and wrong and of true value in all things?

In a real democracy properly qualified public servants would be chosen by lottery and replaced after serving for a predetermined time by others chosen in the same way.

Compare this with the present situation. Nothing can be more important than good government, and yet top politicians in Britain, North America and many other countries need no industrial or commercial experience or other suitable qualifications. They must, however, know how past leaders got away with lies, conniving, corruption and mass murder, and how to inspire such trust and confidence in the general public that their never-ending lies and false promises will not be questioned until they are overtaken by others and forgotten by voters. They must also know how to make part truths more effective than lies, conceal more than they reveal, upset the fewest people possible, and make more and more people dependent on government handouts to ensure their vote in future elections.

Politicians, working secretly and closely with top bureaucrats and their advisers, decide who gets the most profitable contracts.

We could also ask our leaders:

'Why do these always cost taxpayers far more than was originally estimated?'

'Are those who award these contracts bribed?'

'Do their salaries reflect their true income?'

'Is this why their way of life is beyond the means of even the highest paid industrial workers and why ambitious people go to any lengths to win political power and retain it?'

'Is this why every policy of every post World War II British government ended up doing the very reverse of its declared purpose?'

Living standards and quality of life steadily improved before the last war and were very soon beginning to improve again when peace was declared. But our hidden rulers must then have been told that fast developing computers and electronic communications would eventually make it easy to transfer there power to the people.

They therefore decided to reverse direction by transferring our productive industries to low wage countries as a first step in the process of creating an updated version of Orwell's slave world made acceptable by public ignorance of the potential of properly used technology in a completely open society.

The multiplying evils of this policy are concealed by fraudulent government statistics, by cheap imports from low wage countries, by indoctrination with lies, by badly used technology, by sensational newspaper headlines, football, and countless other distractions, and by steadily worsening education.

Comprehensive education, the end of selection by natural ability, the virtual extinction of grammar schools, and laws that make it impossible to discipline children, are essential components of a system that has consigned an entire generation to ignorance of nearly all the cultural and economic issues that contribute to a good and constantly improving life. More and more children are now undisciplined hooligans, more and more will resort to crime.

The extra layers of hugely overpaid bureaucrats and officials who control the European Union have accelerated the decline. The economies of all Member States are being steadily eroded by a ceaseless flood of counter-productive laws. More and more vital industries are transferred to low wage countries, some of which will be allowed to join the Common Market and make matters even worse. Their cheap labour would be free to work in high wage countries and depress living standards even further.

With a system of transparency and moral integrity, this crazy system can be turned on its head and we can all live a prosperous life.

Chapter 9

MEDICAL PRACTICE MADE PERFECT

Doctors don't tell us that normal blood contains traces of all endemic diseases, but we can keep them under control if we are not excessively stressed. If our immune system is given the vitamins and many other substances it needs to do its job properly, we are safe. All the vitamins and minerals we need are provided in a sufficient variety of organic food.

At one time all fresh food was free from chemicals and poisons, and all medications were natural. Nearly all food now contains traces of dangerous chemicals and nearly all medications are now refined chemicals to which bacteria quickly become resistant. This applies no less to natural remedies, if the primary constituent is refined.

Aspirin, for example, is derived from Meadowsweet and is used to reduce pain and thin the blood, but it can cause stomach ulcers and can weaken the immune system. Yet Meadowsweet in its unrefined form has no side effects and strengthens the immune system.

Experience now proves that all man made drugs and refined natural remedies weaken our resistance to disease and are now creating new diseases for which there may be no remedy. But this crucial information is suppressed because making money is now the sole purpose of all activities.

Good health is very profitable for us, but it is not profitable for manufacturers and suppliers of medications, wheelchairs, and the many other necessities of sick people. Bad health is good for them and creates millions of jobs for nurses, doctors, and so-called carers who could otherwise use their wonderful talents to produce more and more of the good things of life and give them much higher living standards and quality of life.

An encounter with an elegant lady who was attending a conference sponsored by a major Pharmaceutical Corporation was illuminating. I entered a lift in which she standing with several delegates. I asked her if she knew that man-made drugs and inoculations cause more deaths and suffering than munitions. She replied "My husband is a very good doctor and he agrees with you, but he can do nothing about it."

Medical practice was the most ethical, loved and respected profession until pharmaceutical producers and distributors realised that bad health is far more profitable than weapons of destruction. Doctors were easily persuaded that synthetic drugs are better than natural drugs because long term deadly side effects may not be revealed by laboratory tests, or they are suppressed by well paid experts. Proven benefits of natural substances are disputed or denied, the most important being that diseases cured naturally strengthen our immune system, whereas cures by unnatural remedies weaken it, and is why medical practice now does far more harm than good.

There is a natural cure for every normal disease, if we know where it is.

On the plus side are safe anaesthetics, miraculous diagnostic machines, and complex surgery which have vastly improved the quality of life for millions of people.

On the minus side are '"miracle drugs"', antibiotics and inoculations which undermine the health of thousands of millions and make us old, infirm and dependent on drugs long before our time, and which now develop diseases for which there may be no remedy.

Statistics make us believe that public health is far better now than in the past because we live longer, but the true reason is totally ignored.

Poor families lived in appalling conditions and ate food that would poison us today. Commonplace diseases were frequent and unavoidable. Hygiene was appalling, food rotted rapidly, sewers were non-existent, garbage, excrement and filth were dumped anywhere. Rats, flies, and other pests were everywhere. The stench in towns and cities was often overpowering. Clean water was scarce, infant mortality, cancers and all other virulent diseases had to be far more numerous and deadly than they are now. Millions were worked to death or poisoned by their jobs before middle age. Children slaved in filthy ships, mines and sweat shops.

We would be dead in a few weeks were our living conditions one tenth as bad as they were for them. Life expectancy may have gone up, but we no longer have their resistance to disease. And in reality, people who ate good food and kept themselves and their homes clean usually lived to an active old age, even in medieval times.

Arthritis and other complaints were unavoidable in those days, but few were completely disabled until old age. Lawyers and other professionals who lived sensibly and did not overeat, drink too much alcohol, or exposed themselves to the stress of living beyond ones means, lived longer than most present day hard working professionals.

Natural remedies were the norm. It is as well to remember that seventy years was the biblical life span 3500 years ago without man-made drugs, inoculations, wheelchairs and other modern marvels! The normal life span of the Essenes of ancient Judea was 90 -100 years or even more!

Ours should be even longer and should be active and healthy until we die, but public health is worsening instead of improving.

Children who died from a common disease would be unlikely to live long anyway. Experience proves that people who survive many illnesses when they are young, and live sensibly thereafter, usually live to a ripe old age.

Experience proves that inoculations and chemical drugs seriously weaken the immune system and that properly fed and reared children do not need them to prevent normal diseases.

European sailors, who first landed on foreign territories with very different climates, sometimes decimated the native population. Native diseases often killed discoverers and settlers. But it must be clearly understood that diseases endemic in other climates must be prevented by inoculations to be safe. The after effects should be minimised by taking more natural vitamins.

Every honest nutritionist knows that genetically modified food and hormones fed to poultry, farmed fish and cattle to make them grow faster are dangerous, and that chemicals added to make food tastier or last longer are making us obese and prone to premature disease. More people are kept alive in misery by the drugs that have done them so much harm every year. Drug producers make immense profits for creating misery.

Account must also be taken of the dreadful obesity and other poisonous effects of junk food, excess sugar, poisonous residues and preservatives in so much of the food now eaten. There is no other rational explanation for the massive increase in autistic children, asthma sufferers and other chronic diseases, but the invariable disclaimer is 'You can't prove it'.

The harsh facts of life and the balance sheets of those who produce or provide man made drugs and pesticides speak for themselves.

Human blood contains viruses of all diseases common to our climate, but a healthy immune system controls them if it has an ample supply of the natural vitamins, trace elements and other blood nutrients to which it is accustomed.

Disease viruses are destroyed faster than they can multiply if a healthy immune system receives the required nutrients. Very few doctors know this, but many are now increasingly aware of the fact that our resistance to disease is reduced by man-made antibiotics and animal serums that are injected into the blood, and that diseases can develop and may not become apparent for many years, before it is too late.

Pasteurization was necessary in days of hand milking and poor hygiene but this now does far more harm than good.

Diabetes was virtually unknown; asthma was extremely rare in rural areas; cancers and other deadly tumours were far fewer among the middle and upper classes in days gone by. These and HIV or AIDS are now the most prevalent diseases and are still increasing.

Improved hygiene and living conditions virtually eliminated tuberculosis, diphtheria, smallpox, syphilis and other deadly diseases, but much more virulent forms are appearing and multiplying.

More people die of heart failure and cancer than ever before.

Millions of people of all ages, who should be healthy and active until they die of old age, are now dependant on mobility aids of infinite variety and on increasingly powerful drugs to which viruses quickly become immune.

Even very young children are now hooked because pharmaceutical producers now control medical practice and dictate the syllabus in nearly all medical schools. Conferences provide free luxury holidays for medical practitioners. Abundant free samples are available. Research "findings" show miraculous cures. Harmful side effects are concealed. Attempts to expose this are crushed.

Thousands of failures are not mentioned or they are attributed to natural causes. The occasional death of a user of a natural remedy, however, makes newspaper headlines, even though it is rarely the remedy's fault.

But times are changing. Doctors can now see what is happening and why, and they must now make their voices heard by all people everywhere.

The primary aim of nearly all medical research would then be to find better ways of using natural methods for preventing and curing disease and to further improve surgery.

The forecasts of many leading medical experts show how wrong well-paid experts can be. Leroy Burney, Surgeon General of the United States of America, David Cox, President of the Kentucky Medical Association, and a host of other physicians jointly declared in the late 1950's that 'the advent of the antibiotic era marks the end for all time of epidemic disease.' Sir F. Macfarlane Burnet, Australian Nobel laureate physician, loudly supported antibiotics and synthetic drugs in 1962. Surgeon General Stewart testified to Congress in 1969 that "it was time to close the book on infectious diseases".

Experience proves that a properly cared for healthy human body resists infection, delays ageing and heals quickly until old age.

All that's needed is a sensible lifestyle and the right kind of wholesome fresh food - half or more of which should be uncooked. Immune systems would then have all they need of the nutrients which protect our health, and to which we are accustomed by millions of years of evolution.

We now eat far too much fat, sugar, salt, chemical additives and preservatives that 'cheat the appetite', a phrase coined by Dr. Cleave, a brilliant Royal Navy physician in his book The Saccharine Disease. This explains simply and clearly why excessive refined sugar is a killer, but the medical establishment ignored his findings.

Cleave noted in his wide ranging naval travels that primitive societies did not develop our diseases and that the common factor was their simple sugar-free, low-fat diets, with honey when this was occasionally available. Diabetes was virtually unknown before cheap sugar was produced.

Countless allergies and diseases continue to multiply, spread, and become more deadly. Excessive refined sugar is obviously responsible for many of our most common diseases, and which lead to other diseases which become more and more serious in a vicious spiral. Animals and humans in the wild eat only as much as they need of their natural food and are never obese or unhealthy until old age, barring accidents or food shortages. Experience also proves that healthy eating habits and food tastes must be cultivated in infancy. A Japanese breakfast would be repugnant to most western people, and yet they are by far the longest living nation and the least vulnerable to disease. But the money profit motive is rapidly worsening their way of life, as it is worsening ours.

Sweets, crisps and other fat-rich snacks and sweetened carbonated drinks should be rare treats until good eating habits are well-established.

Physicians, nurses and other staff can no longer cope with the demands caused by bad food, excessive alcohol, chemical drugs, unhealthy lifestyle, and the stress of ruthless commercial pressures, especially with so much of their time wasted on administration.

This is not a health manual, but good health is so important that a simple explanation of its basic well proved rules is essential, beginning with the fact that two kinds of nutrients are needed to maintain good health, and which are provided by the food we eat if it is varied, good quality and chewed thoroughly.

This is because the nutrients which strengthen our immune system can be dissolved and extracted by saliva and transferred directly into the bloodstream by capillaries in the mouth before being swallowed.

These must otherwise go through the digestive system, kidneys, liver and other vital organs, before reaching the bloodstream, and may even damage the organs through which they pass.

That this makes it easier to digest the food is secondary, but doctors do not offer this information unless we ask. This applies no less to soluble medications.

They can also be transmitted slowly through the skin, or they should be injected if no other way is possible.

The use of animals for drug testing is another worry.

Everyone knows that a given substance may affect different people in different ways. One can only guess how much greater these differences may be between humans and other species.

Two hundred grams of the drug scopolamine is harmless for cats and dogs. *Two grams will kill a human being*.

The amanita haloids mushroom is a health food for rabbits. *One can kill a human family*. There are hundreds of similar differences.

Experience proves that vaccines developed from animals can and often do cause crippling and/or fatal diseases and that one thousand years of vivisection has not produced one cure for human disease. Hans Ruesh describes this as 'legalised massacre' in his book <u>Naked Empress</u>.

Animal rights protesters have good reason to protest the cruelty to animals, but they ignore the far greater cruelty to mankind. All cruelties should be ended as soon as possible.

Nothing can better prove the inherent danger in trying to beat Nature and expose the enormous waste in health care in Britain than statistics for 2002. Administrators employed in the National Health Service had trebled in recent years while nurses decreased by six per cent. £3.64 was spent on administration for every £1 spent on treatments, one-and-a-half hours of which required seven weeks of administration.

That this is worsening and that visitors to hospitals or their doctor's surgery can now pick up new and deadly diseases should no longer be surprising.

Most pre-war British hospitals were small and managed jointly by a head physician and matron responsible to a governing board of voluntary members known as Almoners. Administration costs were minimal, even in large hospitals which could be visited safely at all times.

In 1992, 13,300 hospital patients died of infections that resisted every drug the doctors used. Many more were not noticed or reported. Nor can we know how many more patients were also infected. The true number could be twice as many, or even more.

This is why new small hospitals are now being built for people who can afford private medical practice and do not want to catch hospital diseases.

The criminality of this situation is exposed by the fact that when colloidal silver, a modern version of an ancient anti-biotic, was tested under careful supervision in 1938, it killed several hundred disease bacteria, destroyed harmful viruses and fungi, and did not harm healthy bacteria which man-made drugs are prone to destroy.

No synthetic antibiotic is effective for more than two or three diseases. Nor do any of them destroy viruses or fungi. But this wonderful discovery was suppressed and colloidal silver was not used because it cannot be patented.

To make matters worse, disease bacteria soon becomes immune and new and stronger drugs must be invented to which the bacteria likewise becomes quickly accustomed. These are now creating unknown diseases for which we have no cure, but it has fortunately been proven that bacteria 'forget' their immunity to a given medication if it is not used for three or four years, and makes clear a hitherto carefully suppressed crucial fact of life.

Bacteria cannot become resistant to natural remedies because no two leaves of a plant are identical, and there are far too many different constituents, the proportions of which are different in every batch of natural remedies.

Pharmaceutical producers and their scientists know this. It is a fact.

Increasingly sophisticated treatments for ever worsening diseases demand far greater medical care than ever before, but hospital doctors and nurses, in Britain especially, cannot cope with things as they are.

Far more and far better work could be done with much less effort in an honest world. A mixture of small general and specialist hospitals could give the best possible treatments on demand to whomever needs them. Local, well staffed clinics could provide everyday care for routine individual emergency services that are now available only in very large hospitals, but which often incur very long delays.

Osteopaths, chiropractors and acupuncture specialists could give manipulative and other badly needed natural treatments.

Better food and life quality and natural medications could steadily reduce the demand for physical and mental health care and put an end to waiting lists. Growing leisure would allow time for unpaid social services and relieve the load on medical staff still further and reduce taxes. Helping the sick, the elderly and whoever else needs and deserves help would be viewed as a duty and privilege, and many more people could be active until they die.

All citizens have the right to be protected from avoidable health risks, but having focused attention thus far on the role of medical practice, we can now take account of the damage caused by environmental pollution.

Chapter 10

OH MEDIA, SPEAK THE TRUTH

The mass media would have us believe we have a free press that keeps us fully informed about what goes on in government and big business, but nothing could be more misleading or damaging. Selective reporting of political sleaze makes gullible readers believe they live in an open society, but the massive corruption that really matters is carefully concealed.

The sole purpose of newspapers and magazines is to increase circulation and advertising revenues – at any cost to the public's good. Reporters invade the privacy of newsworthy people and distort and editorialize with a bias nearly everything they say. The result is more confusion and a widespread belief that public affairs are very complex and that no better system is possible, and that sensationalized private affairs are in the public's interest.

Truth in all things would expose the corruption of the present system and make us aware of the fact that it can now be replaced by open, honest and efficient government. As it is, lies and distortions of every possible kind are never questioned. More and more cherished freedoms are destroyed without protest every year. We believe what the propaganda machine tells us.

Most present day readers have been made so blind to what is happening that they read only sensational headlines and think only about bargain offers.

Even the editors, reporters and other contributors have been fooled by our all-powerful rulers. They too have come to believe that consumption, greed, secrecy and lies is the best we can do to race ahead of the pack.

What could be more damning than a Florida Court of Appeal decision in 2003 that there are no written rules against distorting news in the mass media? Newspapers and broadcasters could lie and distort news reports openly if this is allowed!

Crude commercials make everyone want more and more for doing less and less. Celebrities are our role models and idols. They are put on a pedestal by the media machine, and the truth of the matter is, they are there only to sell newspapers, magazines and commercial space on television.

Newspapers distract attention from those facts of life that matter most. Vital information of every possible kind is withheld to prevent our knowing what is happening. But the media must soon change direction.

Increasing production costs and diminishing revenues are creating losses that cannot be sustained. The potential for good can no longer be concealed because information of every conceivable kind is now too easily obtained to silence everyone, and people have started suffering so much that they are starting to listen to reason for the first time.

Truth and openness in all functions and in all walks of life must soon prevail. A growing economic crisis, and the knowledge that newspaper and broadcasting staff at all levels will quite soon lose their jobs and security will compel them to turn on its master.

One United World News Agency would put an end to the harassment of well known people by tens of thousands of superfluous reporters and journalists, all of whom would be employed more usefully, more profitably, and with much more job satisfaction by reporting the truth for the good of every one.

The media, including commercial broadcasts and all other major industries, would eventually be acquired by governments at generous values and liberated from the ruthless pressures of commercial advertising.

Everyone would be correctly informed of world events, economic progress, new developments, cultural and sporting events, trends, holidays, and all other issues of public interest. Major sporting events would be free for everyone to view on screen and would cost only a fraction of what it now costs to attend. Non-commercial advertising would highlight essential issues and help people choose products that are most suited to their needs. None would pander to our self-destructive impulses. Nor would television and radio programs be corrupted by unprincipled commercialism. They would be far more intelligent and stimulating.

Pornography, foul language and unnatural violence would be banned.

Chapter 11

FARMING & FISHING

The importance of farming cannot be exaggerated, but no industry is worse treated, in Britain especially, as evidenced by prices paid for farm produce in recent times.

My elder brother Myer ran away from our very unhappy home when he was sixteen, found work as a farm hand, fell in love with the farmer's daughter and went to Canada for a few years to earn more money and get more experience. He later returned to marry his love and establish his own smallholding. He eventually worked his way up to 105 acres of arable farm on an estate near Truro owned by Lord Falmouth, who attended all family weddings.

Myer made a good living with the assistance of his entire family, whose working week was rarely less than seventy hours, and retired in 1984. He did not drink, smoke or gamble and did more good for society than could a thousand lawyers, bankers and speculators combined, but he did not die a rich man – only a dignified man.

The situation for small farmers today is even worse. Myer's last crop of barley and wheat fetched £96 and £107 per ton respectively. Prices ruling eighteen years later were £55 and £66 per ton with a subsidy that made very little contribution to this shortfall and took no account of inflation and other enormously increased costs!

Reduced revenues, higher farm rents, huge increases in wages and the cost of fertilizers, tractors, other agricultural machinery and equipment, are made ten times worse by an ever-growing mountain of bureaucratic paper work. Most of our small farmers are struggling to make ends meet, and yet they contribute more to society than do all our economists, lawyers and politicians combined.

A dairy farmer in 1970 could make a reasonably good living with a herd of thirty cows. A herd of 150 cows or more would rarely make ends meet now!

It is a fact that many farmers get more for <u>not</u> growing food.

But there is now a much more criminal situation which doctors, politicians and bureaucrats deliberately ignore, and which threatens to destroy our health. Obesity is now the most deadly of all diseases because it is totally ignored.

Hormones that increase weight for a given amount of food are now included in feeds for pigs, poultry, store cattle, lambs, sheep, farmed salmon, trout and other fish and are destroying what is left of our immune system. But no one seems to care!

Insult is added to injury by supermarket buyers who are compelled to reduce prices so much that most farmers now live from hand to mouth. They also make life more difficult by demanding uniformity in the appearance of fruit and vegetables which increases costs and lessens nutritional value.

Harmful pesticides and other chemicals make things even worse again.

But no one can be blamed. The system makes them buy as cheaply as possible and they must make the products look as attractive as they can.

Nothing could better illustrate the appalling evils of our present outdated system and the imperative need to abide by the laws of nature in all things. All people should be told that farmers should be sensibly rewarded and that the best quality can be had only if appearance is secondary to nutrition.

But what is really frightening is that government food experts, who approve genetic engineering to breed disease-resistant crops, know all of this poses enormous dangers to future generations. But they too must do as they are told - or else! Some so-called experts now tell us that properly composted animal manure can be more harmful than chemical fertilizers!

Cloned sheep from long lines of healthy stock are now known to be much more prone to disease than normal sheep. Foods containing animal products caused the *'mad cow disease'* which began in Britain in February 2001, and may still not be ended. This was the inevitable result of bureaucratic rules and regulations framed by the self-seeking, arrogant and immensely overpaid bureaucrats who rule the roost in Brussels and who are yet another unwanted and hugely expensive bureaucracy.

These people are above the law. They can retire on excessive pensions long before the effects of their criminal decisions are visible. Repeated warnings by veterinary experts and independent researchers have stressed the fact that the damage caused to the immune and genetic systems of animals may not show for many years, and that it is even more difficult to detect in humans.

Nothing could better illustrate the appalling evils of our present outdated system and the imperative need to abide by the laws of nature in all things.

It has been known since ancient times that scavengers can digest any food, fresh or rotten alike, that carnivores cannot properly digest vegetation, and that herbivores cannot digest even the freshest meat. Diseased meat must therefore be a deadly poison for cows, as is proved by the fact that this practice created a disease that can disappear only if no such food is given to herbivores for several years.

The quality and honesty of so-called "expert" advice can be judged by the fact that government experts knowingly approved them for dairy farmers!

All farmers could produce organic food safely, economically and efficiently and be paid what they are worth, if our affairs were properly and honestly managed. That some food now grown may have traces of up to 240 pesticides and other chemicals is because they have no alternative.

Agriculture is the lifeblood of most nations. Farm workers' skills are much more valuable and more difficult to acquire than are those needed to make money or keep criminals in circulation and should be properly rewarded.

The demand for organic food is growing fast, but it will be much too expensive for most consumers until the system is changed. Organic farming must be official government policy and buyers should not dictate prices to farmers. In a balanced system, everyone could afford the additional cost, having so much more spending power.

But better health for consumers and better rewards for farmers are not the only reasons to bring about this change. The savings in pesticides, fertilizers, machinery and other expenses would be enormous. And there are many other benefits. It is more labour intensive, hence jobs, and it demands more diversified skills to cope with the greater variety of crops and prevent crop disease naturally.

All worthwhile change takes time, but over time we would see a much larger rural population employed locally, taking the strain of energy consumption and over-crowding in the cities. Rural communities would be practically self-sufficient. They would have top quality schools, hospitals and public transport, good homes, better roads, and numerous comprehensive leisure centres.

Good farm agricultural land would no longer be taken out of production.

Food imports would be substantially reduced.

Research for better and cheaper ways of growing crops would encourage the design and manufacture of farm machinery with huge export potential. These and a wealth of other manufacturing and servicing industries would provide an abundance of well-paid, highly skilled jobs. School leavers and graduates in rural areas would have a much greater choice of interesting, challenging and rewarding careers than could be had in most urban areas.

These benefits are easy to see, and yet there is still one other great benefit to a balanced and open system that has thus far escaped our attention.

All plant tissues are composed of carbon extracted from the atmosphere. If all farming were organic, having been made much more efficient and cost effective by modern technology, millions of tons of carbon dioxide would be extracted from the atmosphere and returned to the soil. This would reduce global warming and improve world climates.

There are many other very interesting possibilities. For example, long-term experiments carried out in Israel clearly demonstrate that many organic salad crops could be produced on a continuous basis on conveyors in growing houses with a controlled environment and automated feeding and watering equipment.

Only a tiny fraction of the land and space now required would be needed to produce these and many other kinds of organic food almost anywhere, regardless of climate or land availability.

Radical change is also called for in the fishing industry. Angling has more active participants than any other sport, and yet although everyone appreciates the food value of fish, their crucial role in maintaining a balanced environment is rarely mentioned.

The oceans would be lifeless without fish, but protecting fish and their environment demands universal collaboration that is presently impossible.

Deep-sea trawlers and floating factories are destroying all marine life on many ocean beds. Coral reefs are disintegrating. Long line fishing threatens whales, tuna, marlin and other large edible species with extinction.

But despite a growing awareness of the potential dangers of this life threatening abuse of nature and of the obvious need to repair the damage before it is too late, the present system can do nothing to stop the rot.

Our dependence on beef and pork is a massive problem on so many levels. It is responsible for the destruction of the rain forest, which provides the planet with much of its oxygen. The methane from the intestinal gases ("farts") of the livestock is the number one culprit of ozone depletion.

As recently reported in the documentary "Food Inc.", the mass produced and processed meat that is being consumed by the masses, especially in the developed world, is disease-ridden and loaded with steroids and antibiotics.

We must return to a system of locally produced fruit and vegetable, locally raised livestock, and sustainable fishing. We must return to a mindset of consuming foods that are seasonal. And we must stop over-eating.

The required controls can be agreed and strictly enforced only if all people in all countries can see things as they are. Everyone would then know what needs to be done and how to do this as efficiently as possible.

This is only one of the countless benefits of a World Unifying Party.

Chapter 12

LAW & ORDER

Openness in all public matters is the only guarantee of a just and effective system of law and order. No known information should be withheld. Criminals should no longer be above the law. Solicitors, barristers and judges should no longer be bribed.

We must stand up, be dignified and take responsibility for our actions. No behaviour of an anti-social nature should pass without penalty. All men should be judged equally under the law. A sense of pride and self esteem would then be reflected in a rapid and accelerating reduction in the numbers of laws, lawyers and law enforcers.

We now have two corrupt and complex legal systems. One is for the rich, who can pay extortionate legal fees to lawyers who know their way round the law. The other is for the vast majority of people who have no redress for injury, injustice or fraud unless they are insured or can draw on public funds.

Police in Britain, France, Italy and many other countries increasingly ignore burglary, theft and minor crimes of violence. They have far too much paper work and so many protections for criminals that they cannot cope with fast multiplying crimes. Minor crimes such as burglary are largely ignored.

Crime now pays as never before. It pays the criminals. It pays the lawyers. It pays the corrupt politicians that turn a blind eye. It is a joke, and the sad irony is that law abiding citizens get less and less justice.

The legal profession, as practised in Britain, America and most other countries, has become a legalised extortion racket and a protection society for lawyers and wealthy criminals. This is the inevitable result of it being self-regulating. Lawyers can bend the law to protect crooked lawyers, knowing that their Law Society will protect them.

What was once one of the most honourable of all professions is as corrupt as politics and will become even more corrupt, until the day lawyers are compelled to reveal all known information at all times, and if several never-questioned legal rules are changed.

Proof of innocence should now be necessary, instead of proof of guilt beyond all 'reasonable' doubt – especially when the identity of the perpetrator or perpetrators is known by many honest people and is privately admitted.

We respect the rights of criminals and ignore the rights of victims. Criminals and terrorists can now do such enormous damage to society that known criminals and terrorists should be compelled to prove their innocence.

Even carefully supervised persuasive measures such as truth drugs may be necessary in a new world that depends on knowing the truth. This would spare the lives and/or property of millions of potential victims and help put an end to all terrorism and crime until the benefits of real democracy stop all deliberate anti-social behaviour.

Nor is capital punishment for deliberate murder the abuse of human rights it is claimed to be. Painless death or imprisonment in a fully self-supporting prison for remainder of the criminal's life should be their choice.

Nothing that defies Nature is sacred, not even human life. Our purpose in the Natural Order is no different from that of any other species. Dangerous people should be put out of harm's way and made to earn their keep when they are in prison, unless they are totally disabled. Even diminished responsibility should no longer be excused, which raises the issue of prisons.

Imprisonment now does nothing for victims of crime and is such a drain on resources that building and maintaining sufficient prisons and training the required staff can no longer be afforded. Convicted people who should be locked up are presently allowed to go free. Many prisoners learn more efficient ways of stealing.

Future prisons will be very different.

It is now so easy to teach normal people how to operate a wide variety of modern production machines and equipment efficiently and safely that all prisons could easily be made self-supporting.

Smaller and more comfortable prisons would be like factories with living accommodation and rules appropriate to the different levels of ability and willingness to co-operate with authority. Inmates would be responsible for nearly all administration in most prisons, knowing that their living standards and quality of life would be as good or bad as they choose to make them.

Staff would mainly be for training. Appropriate measures would ensure that neither the prisoners nor their dependants would need public money to support them. Escape would be out of the question, with nowhere to hide.

The normal working week in the outside world would be constantly reducing and would eventually be less than half its present length, but prisoners would work possibly for sixty hours in a six day working week.

There is no reason to give criminals the same human rights as their victims when all people can have a constantly improving life.

An hour might be spent daily doing physical exercises, with an hour between shifts for lunch.

After work leisure time would include a discussion on current affairs.

Pay rates would be as in the outside world. Earnings would pay for the maintenance of the prison and prisoners' dependants, recompense victims or their families if they were harmed, and provide essential pocket money for inmates. The more they earn, the sooner they could return to normal life equipped with new skills and knowledge. Few would commit further crimes.

One day weekly could be shared with visitors. Some could stay overnight at prescribed intervals. 'Hard case' prisoners would be housed in special prisons with very strict discipline, harsh working conditions and less attractive food until they come to heel, but these would also be self supporting as best they can.

Prisoners who prefer to die should be assisted, there being no good reason to prevent them. Incurable useless mental cases would be peacefully put to death by common consent and under proper supervision, unless relatives or friends agree to care for and control them effectively.

Narcotics and other unhealthy products could not be obtained, grown or used without immediate exposure.

Drug addiction would be very rare because most people are driven to drugs by ignorance, boredom, instant 'kicks', unemployment, poverty, or pressures that could not exist in a real democracy. The craving can become so desperate that they would go to any lengths to get more. Suppliers proliferate because narcotics can be sold for a thousand times more than they cost to produce. Even law enforcers may be bribed.

Fines and 'hauls' by customs are useless. A thousand kilos get through for every kilo found. Convicted carriers are quickly replaced and evasion costs passed on to users. Drug barons are now effectively above the law.

Narcotics addiction is now as big a threat to organised society as miracle drugs, terrorist bombs, chemical antibiotics and inoculations with dangerous serums combined, but this could now be remedied easily.

The simple and obvious solution is to sell them through pharmacies at prices that make illicit trading unprofitable, backed by free rehabilitation centres in convenient locations, and by doctors warning users of the risks involved when they prescribe addictive drugs.

Everyone would be routinely tested periodically; all children would know the devastating effects of narcotics.

Addicts could have only menial jobs, no matter how talented they may be, but they would be imprisoned only if they pose a serious risk to society.

The only statutory drug related offence would be to induce people to take narcotics, unless this is to relieve pain or other specific ailment.

Everyone would carry forge-proof means of identification.

All social experiments involve risks, but few would be tempted in a completely open society which offers a good life to all citizens and has effective deterrents against anti-social behaviour of any kind.

The most powerful opposition to liberalisation may initially come from the police, customs officials and other law enforcement agencies because their immediate reaction could be that they would lose their relatively good and secure jobs, but little thought should now be needed for them to realise that they would have far better jobs and far better lives.

Chapter 13

FOREIGN POLICY

The world is now too small, too interdependent, and too easily destroyed by terrorists and wars to allow politicians, munitions producers and ruthless commercial pressures to determine foreign policy.

We cannot pretend that oppression, false imprisonment, mass torture, and the mass killing of innocent people is not everyone's business. But we cannot use this as any kind of excuse to wage war, when in truth, war is a dirty business that only creates a different kind of havoc in the region, and serves to enrich the oligarchs and strip our economies of any surplus it might have.

The war in Iraq has been costing the United States of America an estimated $1billion per day. Over the course of seven years that adds up to $2.5trillion.

The reported US deficit in 2010 was $1.71trillion.

"Who and where are our enemies?"

The British Aerospace 1991 company report showed that four fifths of the company's profit was made on the two-fifths sales of military and space equipment. Destructive products were six times more profitable than useful ones, but even this understates the true amount. Products can be classified as non-military if only 1% would be used for peaceful ends. Balance sheets are as easily manipulated as government statistics.

Even the Stockholm International Peace Research Institute (SIPRI) seriously understates the production of munitions.

A 1989 report showed USA weaponry production to be nine per cent of the country's GNP, with a further two per cent unrecorded for various reasons. This was half the nation's stated output of manufactured and other consumer products.

Tremendous quantities of munitions are falsely classified to escape embargoes, or they are "legally" recorded as non-military because a tiny proportion may be used by staple industries or service providers.

Recorded weaponry production in Britain was seven per cent of GNP, but a much larger proportion was unrecorded. As manufactures officially accounted for less than 20% of GNP, it is almost certain that the actual proportion of munitions produced was much the same as in America.

The British economy is now so dependent on munitions, that although British exports for 1992 were one twentieth of world trade, they included one fifth of recorded global exports of munitions! These are paid for by imports of food, raw materials, or manufactured consumer goods produced increasingly in low wage countries. The situation has steadily worsened since then.

Bearing in mind the vastly different wage levels, it follows that every job in munitions destroys up to ten jobs in useful industries, but none of this appears in government statistics.

Even the grossly misrepresented Middle East conflict that is destroying so many Arab and Israeli lives and ruining their economies could not be fought without munitions. It is moreover fought because the Arab leadership is determined to preserve its power and privilege by spreading feudalism, and because Israeli politicians are also totally corrupted.

Emotive false declarations of good intentions and the will of Allah is all villainous claptrap. But it is not only the Arabs. Israeli politicians and rabbis are now also corrupted by the system and the true purpose of Judaism has gone down the drain.

Foreign policy of all nations under a World Unifying Party will be focused on bringing real cooperation, real peace, and real democracy to all nations and all regions in dispute. All people will be well-fed, educated and exposed to the good things of life. Everyone will share the same motive: to protect this great new way of life. There will be peace, true empathy, compassion, tolerance and mutual support in a world fit to have and give all children a life far better than in our wildest dreams. What can be better?

Chapter 14

A SMOOTH TRANSITION TO THE BEST WAY OF LIFE

The transition from peace to war in 1914 and 1939 clearly showed us that we will gladly change the way we think and behave and the way we manage our affairs, as and when it is necessary for survival. We are, after all, pragmatic.

A new way of life will unite all nations and make everything constantly improve until the end of time on this planet.

There can no longer be the slightest doubt that everything that happens is predestined and that we have come to the time in our evolution at which we have gathered enough technology, skills, and knowledge of what is good and what is bad, to fulfil the true purpose of our wonderful brains, bodies, and unique free will. Having got this far, little thought should be needed to know that no price can be too high to learn how to fulfil our true purpose in life.

A self-financing World Unifying Party will soon be formed to contest all government elections. These elections will be held with a mandate to end all secrecy, corruption, wars, religious and ethnic hatreds, and form a world co-operative in which all people will be life members.

All privately owned land, mines, forests and established industries would be acquired at a sensible valuation, as and when this is convenient. All industries would be made increasingly efficient, productive and very much more intrinsically valuable.

Payment would be made by United World Government Bonds repayable at face value after 25 or 30 years. No interest would be paid, and yet this would be the best government investment of all time. Inflation that has made hard earned pensions worthless for many hundreds of millions of people would be replaced by fast accelerating purchasing power.

All government employees would serve for a fixed period of five or six years, having signed a declaration that they fully endorse all the objectives of world government, the immediate purpose of which would be to make every nation's economy as diversified and efficient as its population, climate and other resources allow for the mutual benefit of mankind and the natural environment.

Productivity of only the good things of life would far exceed our wildest dreams, and yet far fewer irreplaceable natural resources would be used. Nearly all products would be designed to be recycled cheaply, and a continuously increasing proportion of the labour force would be employed to provide cultural and physical products and services that use very few irreplaceable resources.

All officials who have served their term, or become incapacitated, would be suitably rewarded, given well paid jobs in unrelated activities, and replaced by lottery from suitably qualified applicants.

Patents and copyright and all other restrictions to productivity would be abolished. A new Ministry for Industry and Trade would reconcile the interests of workers, employers, investors and consumers, stop all conniving and make all government services free of charge. Productivity would very soon increase so fast that all legitimate losses due to the transition could be repaid by government without harming living standards.

The legal structure would conform to the ethical principles of the Mosaic Code, and simple national laws would determine the conduct of every nation's internal affairs, while retaining its unique culture and identity. No law would be enforced when it is not needed. Stealth taxes would be bad history. Common sense local laws would enable communities to do what suits them best without harming more people than necessary. Those who cannot derive benefit from the community's mandate would be fairly compensated.

Making the best possible decisions will be easy when all information about all things and all people is stored in regional and national information centres which are updated daily, protected from interference, and made instantly available everywhere by pressing one or more buttons.

Essential service industries would be de-commercialised and integrated.

Far better public services than we have ever had until now would be provided by less than one quarter of the nation's workforce. More than three quarters would then be employed to research, or to produce or provide an ever-growing abundance of the good things of life.

Industrial experts would evaluate the world's best consumer and technical products and select those most suitable for domestic manufacture by carefully chosen manufacturers and entrepreneurs. Loans and incentives would be provided to purchase machinery and installations, train staff, and produce more and more of a growing variety, quality and quantity of top quality products to meet the requirements of well educated and cultured people.

The enormous cost of commercial rents, local taxes, advertising, product and research duplication will be eliminated, as will the current cost of millions of book-keepers, general office workers, cost accountants and auditors employed by competing producers and service providers. The cost of excessive packaging, special offers, and countless other gimmicks, would rapidly be eliminated with astronomical savings. All avoidable waste would rapidly be reduced and the working week would get shorter and shorter.

Vastly increased productivity, coupled with a massive reduction in government dependants, better public health, and the enormously increased efficiency of all public services, would be reflected in a vast increase in the purchasing power of all incomes and in a growing abundance of wholesome leisure activities. Nearly all homes could eventually be filled with lovely possessions of every possible kind.

Industrialists have everything to gain, no matter how big or small they may be. Top rank overseas producers would establish joint ventures with domestic manufacturers, knowing they would have a guaranteed market, good profit margins (subject to quality and competitiveness with leading overseas producers), and a good return on their investments, after paying the wage and salary and other charges agreed with the Ministry. Profits of overseas investors would be tax free and instantly transferable overseas.

Domestic manufacturers in the forefront of technology would be encouraged to establish similar ventures abroad. Producers unable to match the world's best within a stated time would shut down without losses to suppliers. An ever increasing proportion of our manufacturing industries would produce wholesome leisure products and services, and much more time would be spent using and enjoying them. Technical experts from regional offices would regularly monitor all industries and professions to ensure that they are doing everything possible to improve quality and productivity. Increased productivity would increase leisure time instead of making workers redundant.

'Shop floor' suggestions will be encouraged and suitably rewarded, but nothing will be standard practice until it is proved safe.

Powerful buyers will no longer compel farmers, manufacturers and other producers of useful resources to accept less than a fair market price. The extra cost of organic foods and the general shift to a qualitative demand by all consumers will be balanced out by other savings to consumers.

Nothing will be spent on advertising which may now cost much more that it cost to produce the product. Selling prices will reflect the true cost of production and distribution. Many products now sold at ridiculously inflated prices will cost a small fraction of their current selling price. A wonderful bonus will be our knowing that everything we buy is as good as, or better than it has ever been.

Existing international trading agreements will be reviewed, re-negotiated, or cancelled, but all outstanding contracts will be honoured until expiration. Even a few carefully selected munitions may have to be supplied for a while, but weapon producing factories will be quickly converted to making useful products.

Money transfers overseas will be restricted to profits and to payments for essential imports, tourism and business travel, until world democracy is firmly established.

Participating nations will pool all research and join in a common search to find ways and means of making life better for everyone. More progress will be made in one year than can now be made in ten or more years.

Unlimited supplies of safe, cheap and non-polluting energy will be made available within a few years and it will be imperative that we build water pipelines that will take water from where it is plentiful to where it is desperately needed.

Drug research will be devoted to finding natural remedies and getting to know how best to use them for everyone's benefit.

Imported goods that in time can be efficiently produced at home will be controlled or banned when domestic production is under way and controls are no longer needed.

Manufacturers of agricultural machinery will concentrate on developing labour saving equipment for organic farming and help make it standard practice. Farmers will be given whatever help is needed to complete the transfer from chemical to organic farming. Subsidised energy will enable horticultural producers in northern countries to grow high value unseasonable produce under glass or polythene – that way saving on costs associated with importing fruits and vegetables.

Every effort will be made to ensure that constantly improving education and training makes competent workers of every description freely available.

Management will be so much easier and salary differentials will rapidly reduce. Pay differentials will eventually disappear and money would no longer be needed!

Lump sum severance payments, share options and 'golden handshakes' will be abolished. Redundant workers will have full pay until they are re-employed, even if they need re-training.

Partly disabled people will have suitable jobs and all they need to live in comfort. Pensions will easily maintain established living standards and will keep pace with rising standards.

All privately owned land and house mortgages will be transferred to a National Land Agency and all personal debts cancelled when a sufficient number of industries are restored. Lenders will be fully reimbursed by government. Rent will be charged for land occupied by housing, but this will be very much less than is now paid to landlords, building societies, banks and other money lenders.

Shareholders in public or privately owned companies will be able to exchange their holdings for long term interest free government bonds at an agreed realistic valuation and make it much easier for all industries to adapt to the very different conditions of this new way of life. It will also be far more profitable for industrialists and investors than take-over bids!

Education will help all pupils and graduates to make the most of their inherent ability and special talents, and to acquire the skills demanded by fast increasing technology. Children with special aptitudes will be able to make the most of their gifts, unlike the majority of children today. More and more people will be cultured in the true sense of the word.

A carefully prepared health education program will minimise obesity, encourage a better lifestyle, and improve public health. Sugar based confectionery, those sweetened with chemical sugar substitutes, unhealthy fast foods and foods laden with preservatives and/or chemical colourings will not be allowed for children until they know why good food is all important, and sensible habits are established. In time all unhealthy foods will be phased out.

Far less stress will be reflected in far fewer strokes and cancers.

Human rights will not be an issue in a democratic world. Refugees and exploited workers will be bad memories.

The European Common Market will be disbanded and its members will make their own democratic decisions - without losing their traditions and culture, or losing sight of the objective of making life better for all nations.

Fishing in the territorial limits of other nations without specific permission will be prohibited until this new way of life enables us to readily agree and cooperate on restrictions that benefit all. Sensible controls can then be imposed and baby fish will no longer be trapped in fishing nets. Ocean beds and coral reefs will not be destroyed by pollution or deep sea trawlers.

All land, minerals and industries will eventually be held in trust for the benefit of the entire world population, without harming those who own or control them legitimately. Surplus funds taken by government for whatever reason will be used to promote public well-being and will be publicly acknowledged.

There will be periodic reviews of working hours and conditions, health and safety measures, holidays and all other regulations.

There will be no booms or slumps, labour or working capital problems. No time or effort will be wasted trying to increase market share. Pay increases not matched by cost savings will be banned until a rational income policy is established, but an end to restrictive practices will allow all competent workers to do any job at the going rate.

Incompetent or negligent workers and managers will be downgraded, otherwise, more suitable employment will be made available. The dreadful worries of unemployment, reduced incomes, poverty pensions, huge debts and other evils will also be laid to rest.

Stressful jobs, such as air traffic controllers, will be limited to, say, five, ten, fifteen or twenty years, depending on their nature, with free training for alternative employment without losing pay, benefits, or status.

Prompt payment for goods and services will be mandatory. Bad debts will be reimbursed by government.

Giving bank cheques without sufficient funds or buying goods or services that cannot be paid for will be serious crimes – as it is in some parts of the world already.

Charities will no longer be needed. Abundant resources will cater for all genuine needs and paid charity workers will have far better jobs.

It must be made clear, however, that a tremendous amount of labour will be required to restore the natural environment until world climates are stabilised. Millions of square miles of forests must be replanted; tens of thousands of kilometres of pipelines must be laid to transport water to deserts; ocean beds must be rested until they are properly restored and fish stocks are replenished.

Hundreds of millions of people will be transported from hovels and dreadful city slums, to be properly re-housed, trained, and employed in new industries.

Regular public meetings will encourage discussions and debates about all activities of public importance, but conflicting self-interests such as we have now would be rare, and within an open and honest system will be reconciled peacefully and with the best interests of the community a priority. Continuous improvement in all things will be easy when everyone works openly for a common cause, but allowance will be made for the fact that habits instilled by thousands of years of life in an entirely different environment will not be changed overnight.

If you are one of the many who are convinced that change of this order is impossible, or that money defines a man's wealth, or that it must take many hundreds of years, I beg you to think more deeply.

There are no limits to productivity, but only if fast increasing technology is exploited as efficiently as possible for the mutual benefit of all people. But we must accept the fact that not all nations can join at the same time, and that major changes must be phased in to avoid hardship.

Aid to weaker nations will be given free, for this would be the best investment we can make. All natural resources will then be properly exploited for the benefit of the entire population of this planet for the first time.

Can we adapt to this new way of life? If we look back upon the second world war, nearly two thirds of Britain's adult population became military personnel or war workers. The acquired an adequate working knowledge of machines and processes within weeks or months; knowledge that would have taken years in peacetime. Soldiers, sailors, airmen and civilians resumed their old jobs or found new when war ended. Devastated cities were restored, new industries mushroomed, and the dreadful anxieties of war set aside.

Adaptation is not man's weakness.

Even greater changes took place in Germany and Japan! The colossal task involved in rebuilding post-war Germany defies imagination. The destruction in the Ruhr, Cologne, Hamburg, and Berlin, to name but a few major targets, was far greater than the destruction in all of Britain and France.

The most reputable 'experts' declared that the destruction and other losses could not be repaired in 100 years. Russia tried to make doubly sure by stripping occupied territories of industrial machines and equipment and transporting German scientists and technologists to Soviet laboratories, factories and labour camps. America, Britain and France seized important patents and know-how, and recruited many top brains for their own industries.

And yet despite all this, nearly all this damage was restored within ten years. Ten more years saw West German industries, cities and towns rebuilt better than before. Germany was once more Europe's leading industrial nation.

This shows how little faith we should have in so-called experts and how much can be done if enough people are prepared to work hard.

Britain, as usual in such matters, lagged far behind, even though it had more Marshall Aid than Germany.

But Japan provides an even more striking example of the potential of man to adapt and to use modern technology to improve the standards of a nation. Seemingly backward by Western standards prior to the war, and with two major cities devastated by nuclear weapons, Japan now has the strongest of all economies and the largest per capita **genuine** gross national product in the world. Workers who once lived mainly on rice are among the world's top earners. But professional and executive salaries are low by Western standards. They spend far more on food than any other nation and still have the best technical education and public services and the least crime. Anyone can walk the streets without fear of being robbed, mugged or raped.

A rumoured higher suicide rate is not supported by statistics.

The market value of Japanese productive industries is more than the total value of all Common Market industries. No one knows how much real estate they now own throughout the world. It is far greater than we may think.

They lost the war to win world domination, and won the subsequent war of industrial domination. But the time has come to even things up, for their benefit, as well as for ours. The Japanese people are now also being made increasingly ignorant. All nations are becoming "Americanised".

One cannot visualise the limitless potential for making life better for future generations. We would produce an abundance of everything needed to give all people a constantly improving cultured life.

Crime-infested slums, ghettos and other crude, claustrophobic, alienating and impersonal municipal housing developments will cease to exist. All homes will be fit to live in. Increasingly paranoid security measures will no longer be needed.

Most urban homes will have solar energy panels and well insulated walls, and would comprise mainly three, four or five storey terrace houses with private gardens, balconies, and below-ground car parking and utility rooms. External passenger lifts would serve the upper floors of adjoining homes, many of which would be lovely flats to accommodate elderly people.

Roof gardens, window boxes, floral displays and productive kitchen gardens will be commonplace. Neighbours will get to know and help one another. Children would make friends easily. Privacy will be respected.

Free communal leisure centres equipped with a wide variety of wholesome facilities will be commonplace. Everyone will be able to fraternise and participate in all sorts of interesting pleasure-giving activities that are rarely found in today's commercialised world. Opera, theatre, contemporary dance, live music, cinema, and all other worthwhile entertainment will be affordable to all. Amateurs will have every possible encouragement to perform publicly.

Everyone will have far better things to do than drink alcohol, take hard drugs, gamble, listen endlessly to eardrum destroying music, have random sex, eat junk food, spend hours shopping, watching commercial TV, or generally be useless members of society.

All youngsters will have a proper sense of value and culture. They will be exposed to a broader range of activities, ideas and opportunities to enrich their lives; to truly taste the good things of life.

One income will give a family all they need for health and happiness. Mothers will be able to rear healthy intelligent children and give them the love and care that only full time mothers can offer. Mothers could then provide a second income or do whatever else they choose.

A sense of security in all aspects of a life will put an end to nearly all the frictions and differences that destroy marriages today. It should also put an end to sexual abuse and perversion, and make lasting and happy relationships the norm. Divorce settlements will at worst be peaceful and mutually satisfactory.

Millions of inventive and productive people, presently frustrated by a system that makes it impossible for them to benefit from their knowledge, will be encouraged to establish small productive units that will eventually be acquired by the nation at generous valuations, if they succeed.

This new way of life will mark the end of all charges for government services, the end of all restrictions on justified freedoms, the end of exorbitant interest charges, the end of all security costs, the end of high rents, high business rates, extortionate legal costs and the countless other charges we now pay. This new of life will open the door to a freedom that was commonplace when I was a young man.

Very few individuals can afford to establish a useful business because everything is designed to protect and promote big business and the dictatorship of George Orwell's "Big Brother Slave World".

The will of a Real Democracy is a very different matter for which all sensible people will gladly settle. The purpose of every function of life will be to try to do it or make it better, no matter how good it may already be. No purpose can be more worthwhile.

Please give this the thought it deserves and act accordingly. You have everything to gain and nothing to lose, even if you are a member of one of the hierarchies. Your gain will far outweigh your loss.